It was Monday afternoon at Woodside School.

All the children were working very hard.

Three new children had come to visit the class.

Miss Owen was showing them the classroom.

First of all they went to the book corner.
There were lots of exciting books and there
were three soft cushions to sit on.
One of the new children said,

Next they went to the play corner.
There was a shop and a telephone and
a big box of dressing up clothes.
One of the new children said,

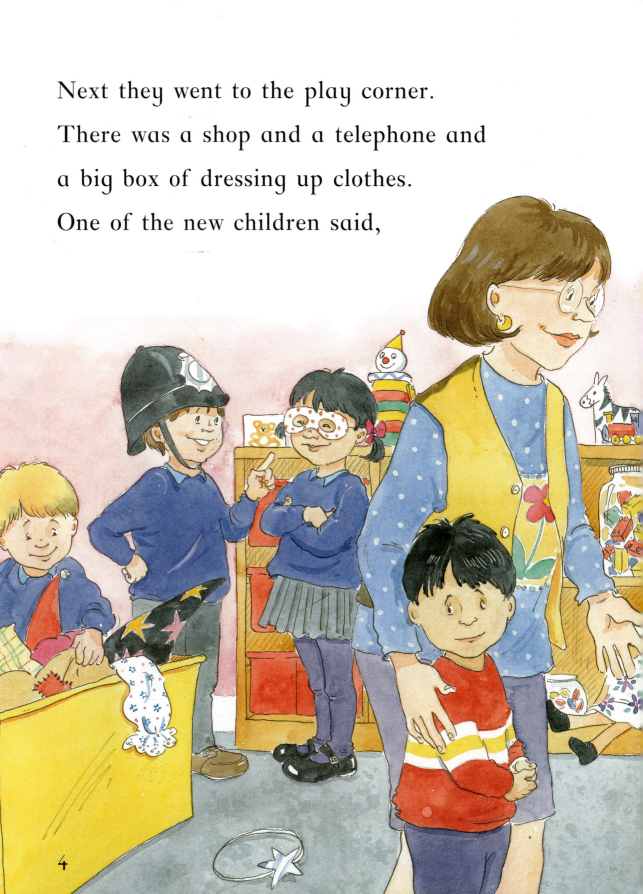

Next they went to the home corner.
There was a cooker and a sink and
a table and four chairs.
The last of the new children said,

7

At the end of the afternoon Miss Owen clapped
her hands and said,
'Girls and boys, it's time to go home.'
'Oh no!' said the new children,

We want to play.